Rig it Right Essentials

Freshwater FISH

CONTENTS

Bass Rigs

CAROLINA WORM RIGS

TIP

The beauty of the Carolina Rig is that it keeps the weight away from the plastic worm or lizard so it can float just off the bottom in an enticing manner

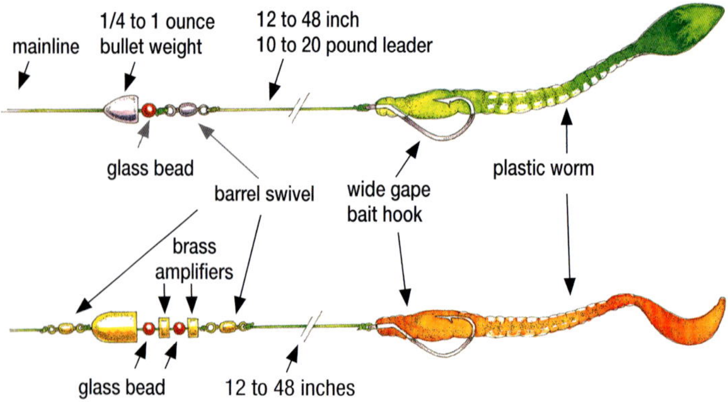

VERTICAL CAROLINA RIG

TIP

Deep water areas and drop-offs can be fished with this heavier rig.

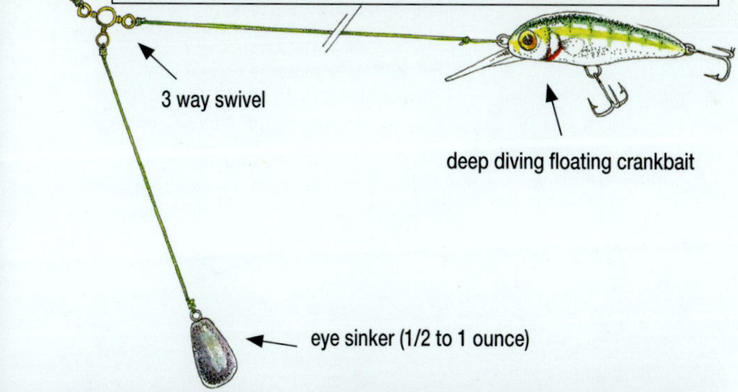

TEXAS RIGS

TIP

Bass tend to frequent areas around structure such as weedbeds, submerged trees, boulders etc, so using any type of lure setup like a Texas Rig that has the hooks concealed is a bonus when it comes to avoiding getting snagged up.

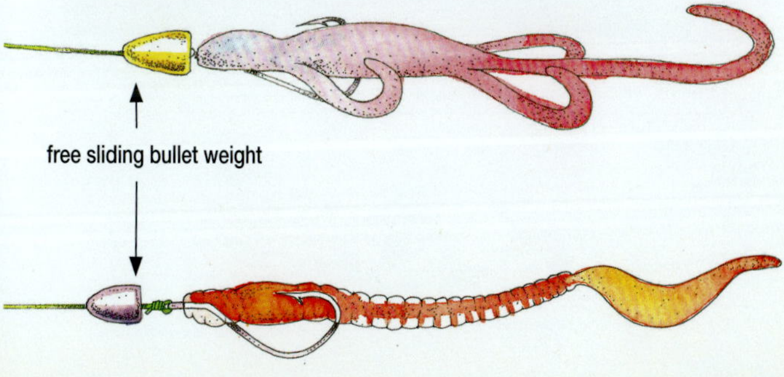

SPLIT SHOT RIG

TIP

This finesse rig eliminates the bullet sinker that is used in a Carolina Rig and uses a split shot to the line. It is a fantastic rig for searching out keeper bass generally holding in water less than 20 feet deep. Use small baits around 4 inches in length,.

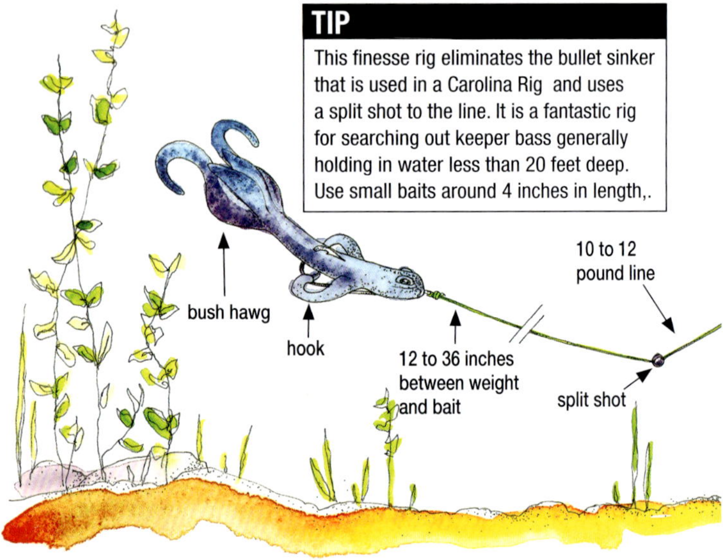

TOPWATER BAITS

TIP

Fish surface baits at both ends of the day and around cover for some fantastic visual bass fishing action. Tie gelspun direct to the lure.

DROP SHOT RIGS

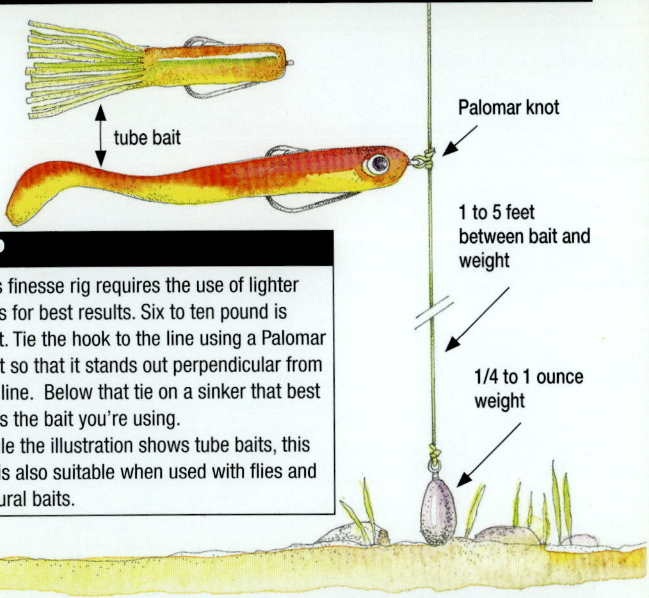

TIP

This finesse rig requires the use of lighter lines for best results. Six to ten pound is best. Tie the hook to the line using a Palomar knot so that it stands out perpendicular from the line. Below that tie on a sinker that best suits the bait you're using.
While the illustration shows tube baits, this rig is also suitable when used with flies and natural baits.

CRANKBAIT

TIP

Crankbaits imitate a variety of prey that bass feed upon, including crawdads fish, and lizards and frogs.

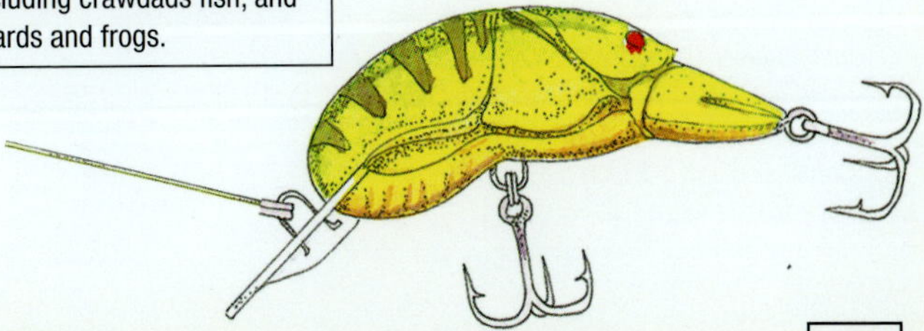

SPINNER BAITS

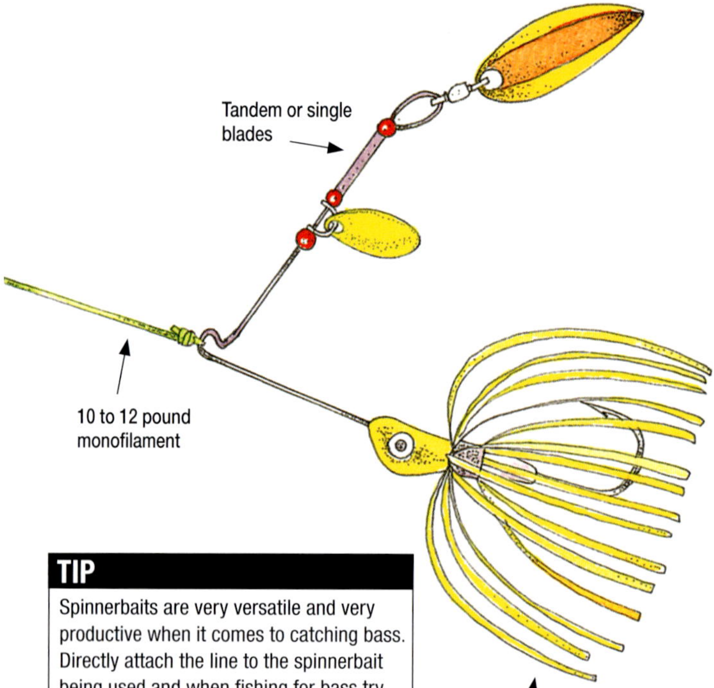

TIP

Spinnerbaits are very versatile and very productive when it comes to catching bass. Directly attach the line to the spinnerbait being used and when fishing for bass try and always keep in visual contact with the lure and don't strike immediately when a bass hits.
Tandem blades can be fished slower and hold higher in the water and gives off more flash than a single blade which does produce more vibration when it's working. Consider using a 3 inch plastic trailer to the hook to give extra fish appeal!

LARGEMOUTH BASS

One of the most popular and sought after freshwater sportfish in the United States. They are aggressive fish that will hit lures, flies and baits with equal enthusiasm. They are an acrobatic fish that offer a strong fight, especially on lighter outfits.

Fishing outfits should reflect where you're fishing. In amongst snags and weedbeds it may be necessary to use heavier lines and stronger outfits to subdue and turn larger fish. Artificial lures such as plastic worms, spinners, top water plugs and jigs are all successful. Fly anglers often use surface popper flies.

Fishing live baits such as crawfish, leeches, frogs, minnows and night crawlers are all successful in various regions of the country.

SMALLMOUTH BASS

A very good (one of the best) fighting fish that are both strong and acrobatic. Because they tend to prefer open water areas they can be targeted using lighter tackle that allows them to put up a better fight. They eat various foods including frogs, insects, crayfish and even small mice.

They are usually fished for with light spin and baitcasting tackle as well as fly tackle where appropriate. They can be caught on a range of natural and artificial baits and lures. Jigs, crankbaits, spinnerbaits, and plastic jerkbaits are all productive as are various wet and dry flies. Natural baits as mentioned above are all successful.

RIGS Walleye

BOTTOM WALKING RIG

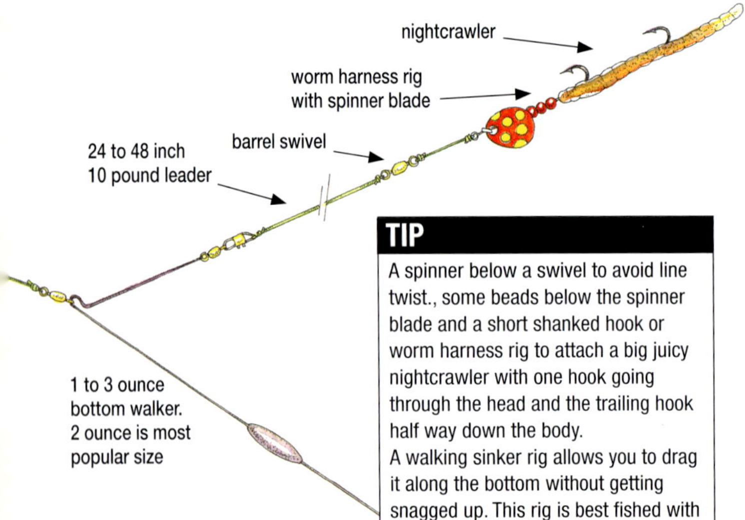

TIP

A spinner below a swivel to avoid line twist., some beads below the spinner blade and a short shanked hook or worm harness rig to attach a big juicy nightcrawler with one hook going through the head and the trailing hook half way down the body.

A walking sinker rig allows you to drag it along the bottom without getting snagged up. This rig is best fished with a drift rather than trolling. Trolling this rig will put walleye in the bag and will work, but many anglers prefer to slow drift this rig.

STAND UP JIG AND NIGHTCRAWLER

TIP

Stand-up Jigs are ideal for both largemouth and smallmouth bass, and when fished with a tube bait (or other soft plastics) they offer a fantastic representation of a defensive crawfish. Add a nightcrawler onto a trailing hook and fish it on a hard rocky bottom or next to a well defined weedbed and get ready for some serious action!

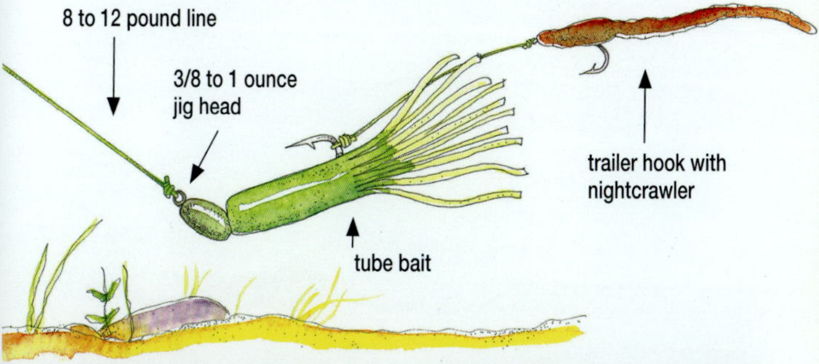

TROLLED PLUG

TIP

Walleye will readily hit trolled plugs.

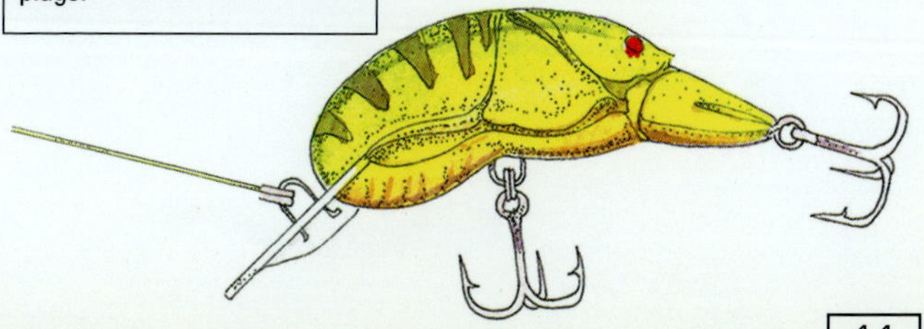

LEECH RIG

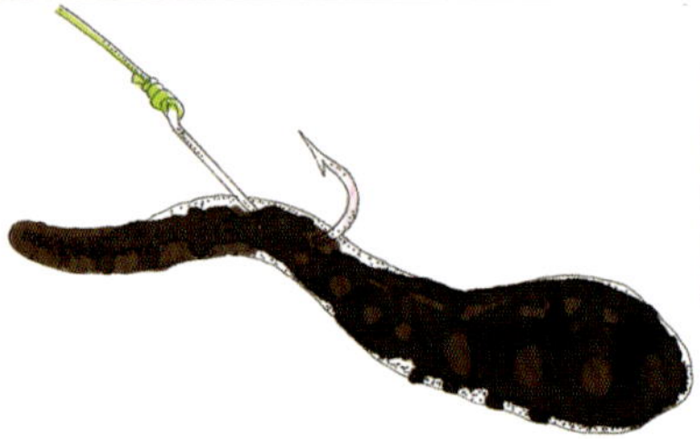

TIP

When fshing a leech hook through the center of body or thick end.

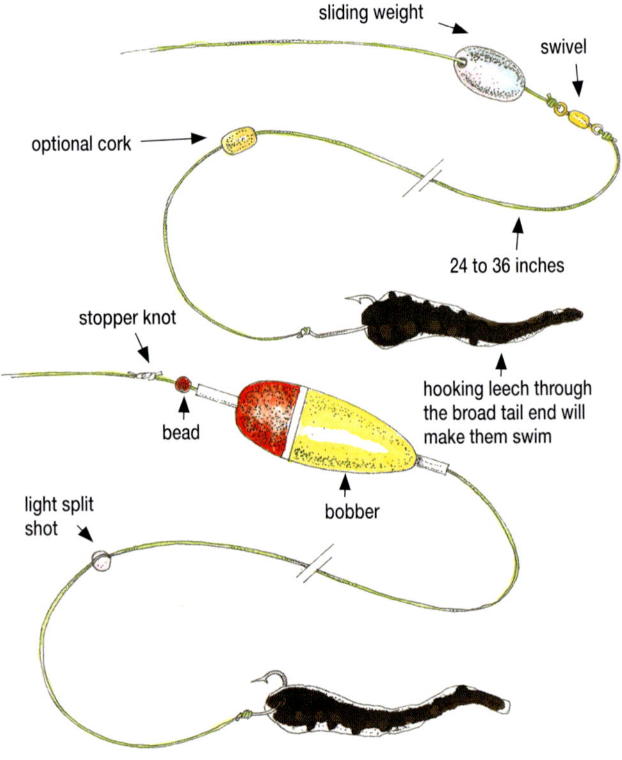

SAUGER

Similar to walleye. They aren't ferocious hitters of baits or lures, and they tend to feed near the bottom. Best fishing is usually during low light at each end of the day. Spinning and baitcasting outfits are the preferred outfits. The best bait is a live minnow, but they will eat worms etc. They will hit various lures including jigs, spinners (especially if tipped with a minnow) and spoons.

WALLEYE

They provide a strong but usually short duration fight. They are probably more valued for their eating qualities, and are generally targeted with spin and baitcasting tackle using natural baits and artificial lures. Natural baits include leeches, minnows, small bullheads and nightcrawlers. Natural baits probably account for most walleye captures. They can be finicky feeders at times, but will hit cast or trolled jigs, crankbaits, spoons and in-line spinners. Trolling is the most effective means of locating fish. Downrigging and lead core lines allow for targeting fish down deep.

RIGS Crappie & other Panfish

JIG AND FLOAT RIG
BOBBER AND MEAL WORM RIG

TIP

Adjust the depth of the hook or jig to match the depth of water and where the fish are holding. Use a few split shots on the line below the float to get light baits into the strike zone or where there might be some current.

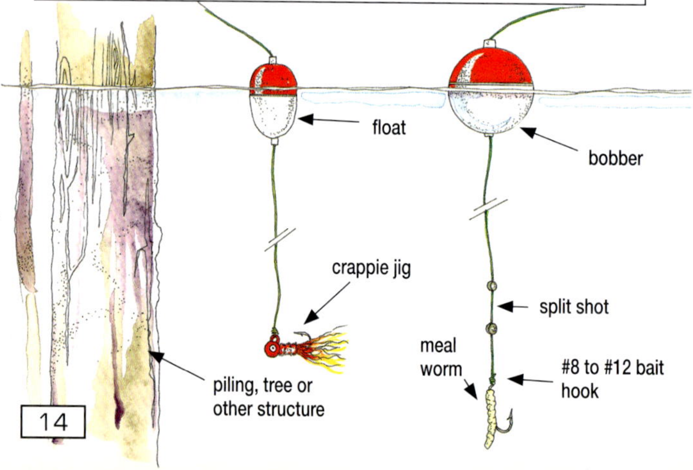

DOUBLE SPREADER RIG

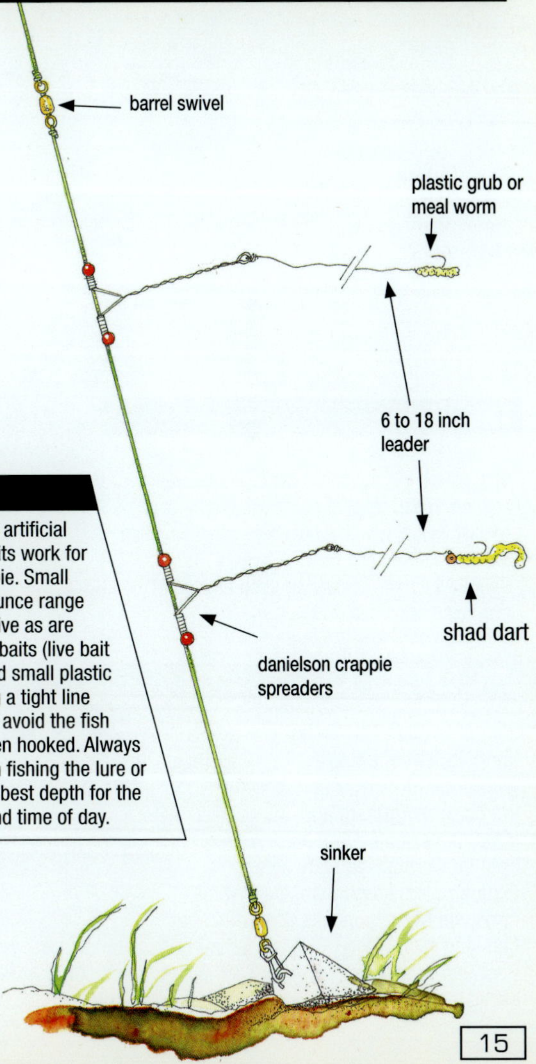

TIP

Any number of artificial and natural baits work for catching crappie. Small jigs in the ¼ ounce range are very effective as are small minnow baits (live bait or artificial) and small plastic grubs. Keeping a tight line is important to avoid the fish getting off when hooked. Always concentrate on fishing the lure or live bait at the best depth for the time of year and time of day.

DOUBLE BEAR PAW RIG

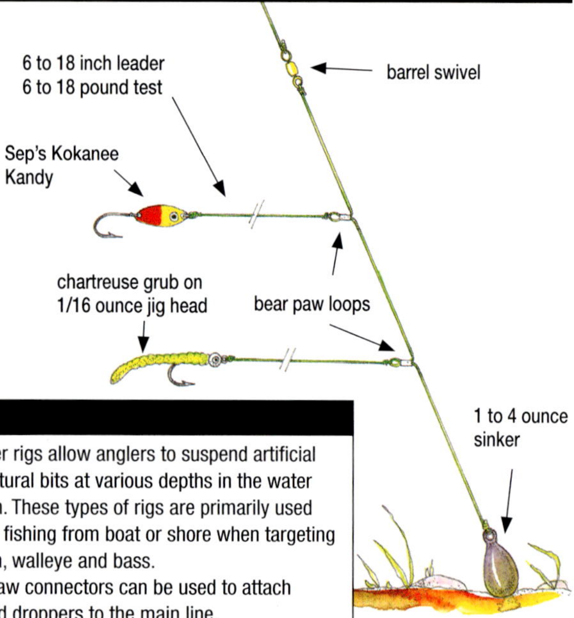

TIP

Dropper rigs allow anglers to suspend artificial and natural bits at various depths in the water column. These types of rigs are primarily used for still fishing from boat or shore when targeting panfish, walleye and bass.
Bear Paw connectors can be used to attach pre-tied droppers to the main line.

BLUEGILL

Lots of anglers 'cut their teeth' catching bluegill and other sunfish. They are scrappy fighters and good fun when caught on light tackle such as spin, fly and fishing poles. They willingly hit small lures, spinners, poppers, jigs small wet flies and nymphs, as well as natural baits such as meal worms, worms, freshwater shrimp, crickets, small baitfish plus corn kernels, bacon and bread dough.

BLACK CRAPPIE

An extremely important recreational sportfish. What it lacks in fight compared to some other panfish makes up for in its eating qualities. Usually targeted with cane-poles or light spin tackle. They are often fished for using small minnows as bait, but will hit other baits such as worms. Small spinners, spinnerbaits, feather jigs and crankbaits are all popular; they will also hit small streamers cast with flyrods. Trolling deepwater with diving plugs, spoons etc is also effective.

WHITE CRAPPIE

Targeted for their eating qualities, rather than their fighting abilities that leave something to be desired. Depending on the season and the location of the fish, poles, spincasting and flyfishing are all productive methods when targeting white crappie. Tiny jigs, doll flies, small crankbaits, spoons, spinners and other lures will all catch these fish, as will flies. Natural baits are probably the most productive however, and the use of live, medium sized minnows is the most successful.

RIGS

Pike-Pickerel & other large gamefish

WEEDLESS SPOON RIGS

TIP

Weedless spoons tipped with pork or soft plastic worms are great baits for fishing fast through lily pad areas.

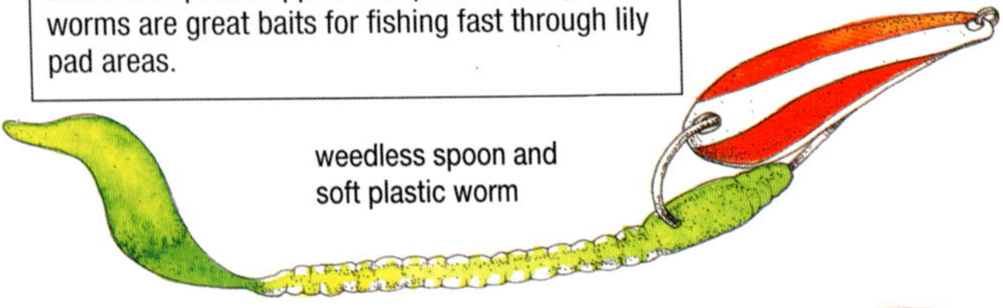

weedless spoon and soft plastic worm

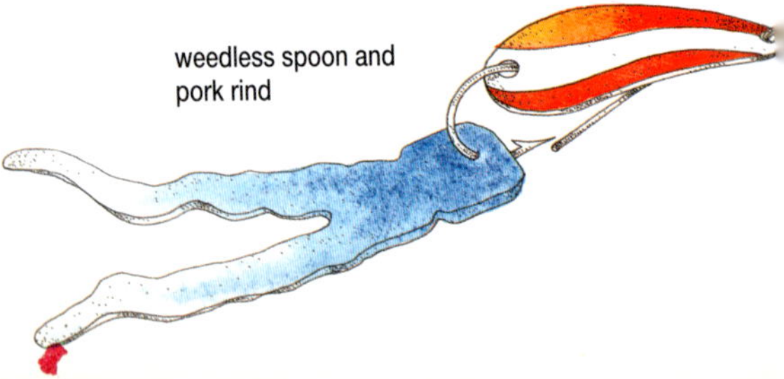

weedless spoon and pork rind

BOTTOM BUMPING RIG

TIP

This rig with the addition of the cork can be used to keep the bait off the bottom when targeting smallmouth bass and catfish.

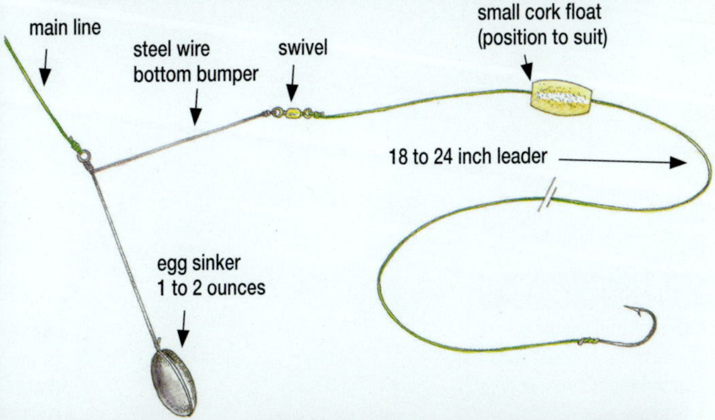

WEEDLESS LIVE BAIT RIG

TIP

Using a cigar float and weedless hook allows you to fish through surface weed vegetation with less chance of getting snagged.

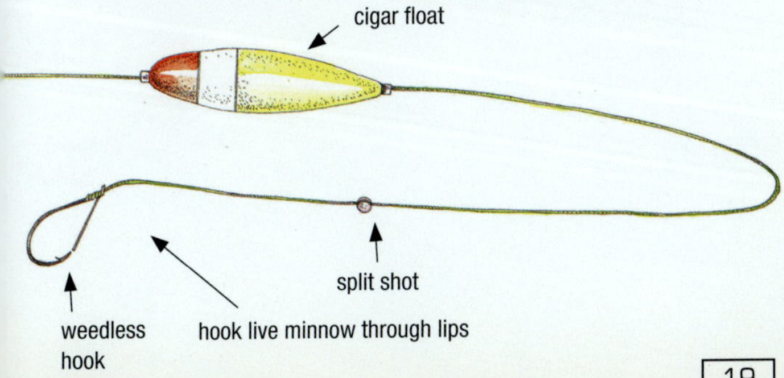

QUICK SET RIG

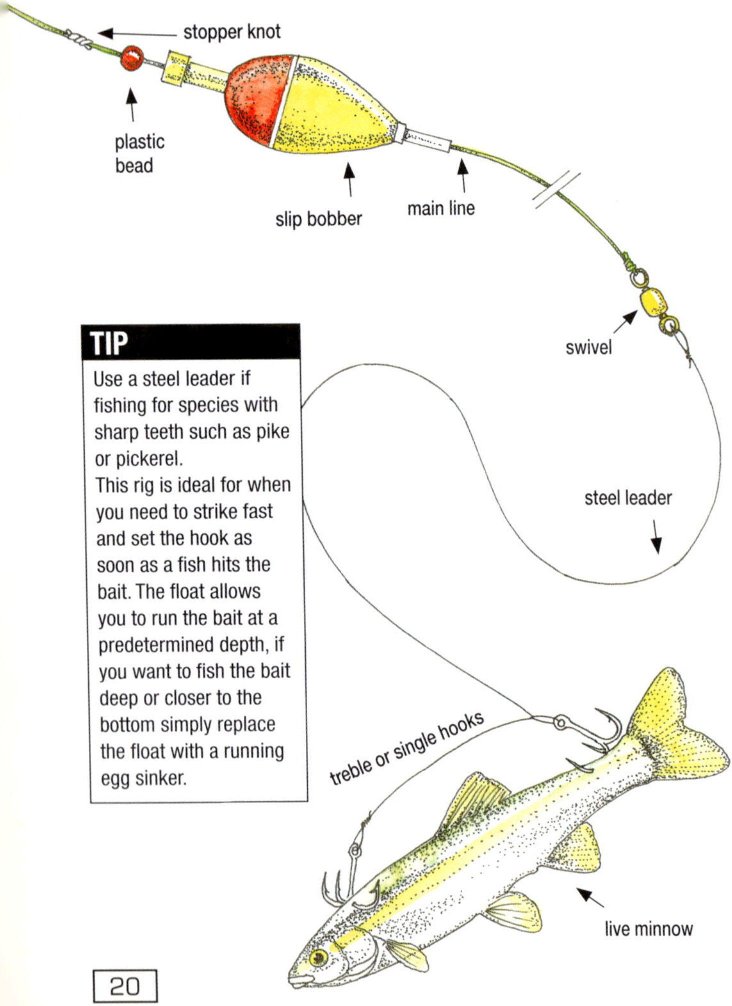

TIP

Use a steel leader if fishing for species with sharp teeth such as pike or pickerel.
This rig is ideal for when you need to strike fast and set the hook as soon as a fish hits the bait. The float allows you to run the bait at a predetermined depth, if you want to fish the bait deep or closer to the bottom simply replace the float with a running egg sinker.

CONTROLLED-DEPTH LIVE BAIT RIG

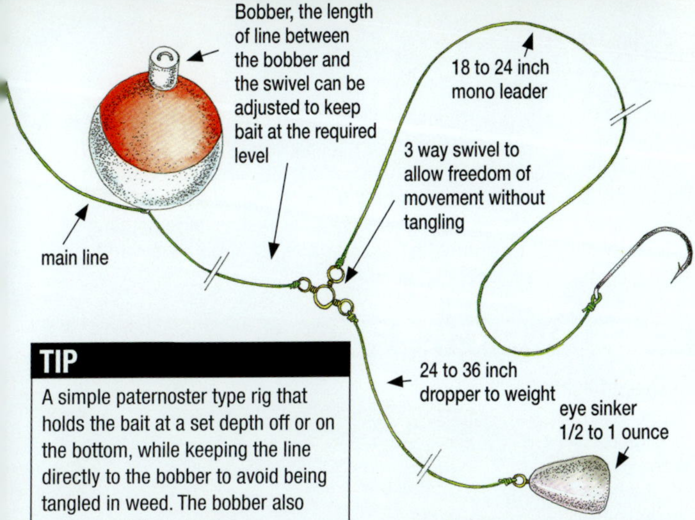

TIP

A simple paternoster type rig that holds the bait at a set depth off or on the bottom, while keeping the line directly to the bobber to avoid being tangled in weed. The bobber also acts as a strike indicator.

MUSKELLUNGE

One of the toughest, they are an apex predator. The fight is usually, strong, violent and acrobatic with head shaking leaps. Quality, strong baitcast, spin or fly gear is needed to subdue these great sportfish. Muskie's don't come easily, and often require numerous casts to elicit a strike.

Live baitfish (around 8-10 inches in length) are top baits, either drifted or trolled. Large, noisy surface plugs are popular, as are jerkbaits and bucktail spinners. Very large lures around 12-20 inches are often used. Flyfishing with large streamer flies can be successful if the angler is prepared to put in hundreds of casts between strikes.

NORTHERN PIKE

A very aggressive fish that fights hard, jumps and runs when hooked. Baitcast, spin and fly tackle are productive on northern pike. They are easier to tempt onto the hook compared to the Muskellunge and tiger musky, and will eat virtually any live baitfish, lure or fly put in their path. They will cannibalise when other fish prey become scarce. They will hit a wide variety of lures, as per muskellunge, as well as large popping or streamer flies. They seem to be more attracted to brightly colored lures and flies than natural colored offerings.

CHAIN PICKEREL

A spirited fighting fish that hits lures, flies and baits ferociously. Best when taken on light tackle. They are often taken by bass anglers casting plugs, but also hit spinnerbaits, spoons, jigs, crankbaits, flies, bucktails and surface plugs. They will eat live minnow baits and pork rind baits.

SAUGER

Similar to walleye. They aren't ferocious hitters of baits or lures, and they tend to feed near the bottom. Best fishing is usually during low light at each end of the day. Spinning and baitcasting outfits are the preferred outfits. The best bait is a live minnow, but they will eat worms etc. They will hit various lures including jigs, spinners (especially if tipped with a minnow) and spoons.

BLUE CATFISH

The largest of all the catfish. Its size alone equates to a serious tussle, even on heavy tackle, but even 'smaller' fish are solid fighters. Trotliners often catch the largest fish. Heavy spin, baitcasting or even light saltwater tackle is not out of place when tackling these big fish. They will take numerous baits including live (or dead) fish such as herring and shad, large cut baits, pieces of meat, crayfish and prepared baits.

BROWN BULLHEAD

Offer a reasonable fight on light tackle. Most anglers use poles or spin tackle. They will take baits such as worms, shrimp and minnows. Also stinkbaits, cheese, bread dough and chicken liver. Although they are night feeders, anglers do catch them throughout the day.

CHANNEL CATFISH

Will take artificial lures but is rarely deliberately targeted with anything other than baits. Usually caught using heavier spin and baitcasting outfits for bigger fish and lighter outfits and poles for small specimens. Popular with trotliners where legal.
They will take most baits, live and dead baitfish, crawfish, cut baits, worms, dough balls, liver, chicken innards, cheese, crickets, grasshoppers and stinkbaits. Also 'noodled', a method where the fish is caught by hand. States where this practice is presently legal are Mississippi, Alabama, Arkansas, North Carolina, Missouri and Georgia.

RIGS Sturgeon

SLIDER WITH SHRIMP RIG

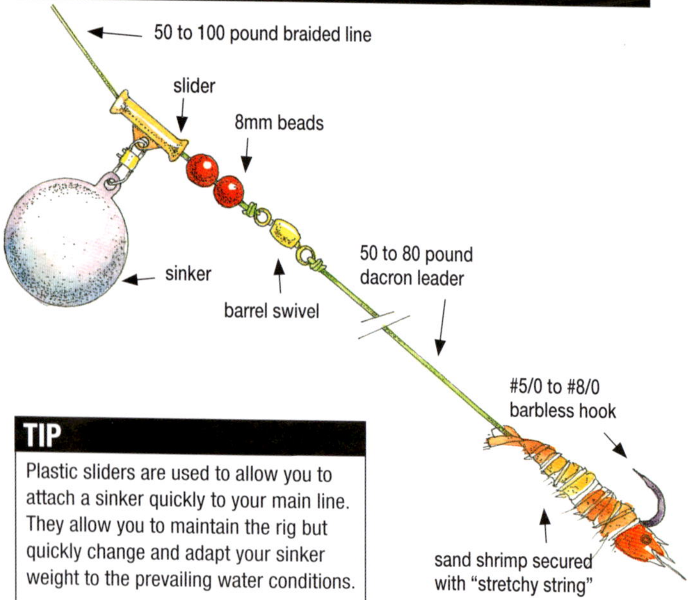

TIP

Plastic sliders are used to allow you to attach a sinker quickly to your main line. They allow you to maintain the rig but quickly change and adapt your sinker weight to the prevailing water conditions.

SLIDER RIG WITH HALF HITCHED SMELT

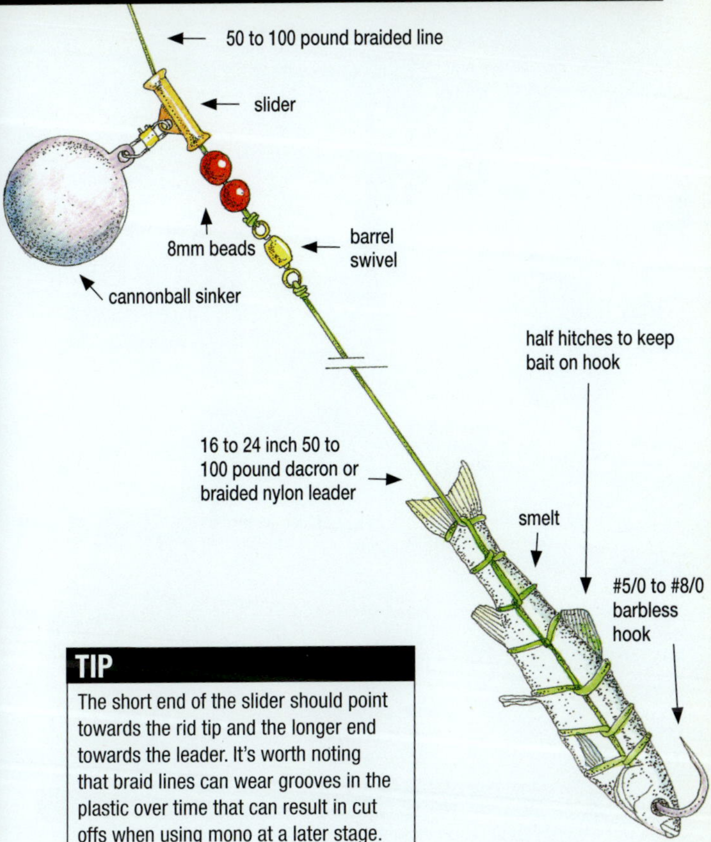

TIP

The short end of the slider should point towards the rid tip and the longer end towards the leader. It's worth noting that braid lines can wear grooves in the plastic over time that can result in cut offs when using mono at a later stage.

SEWN SHAD STURGEON RIG

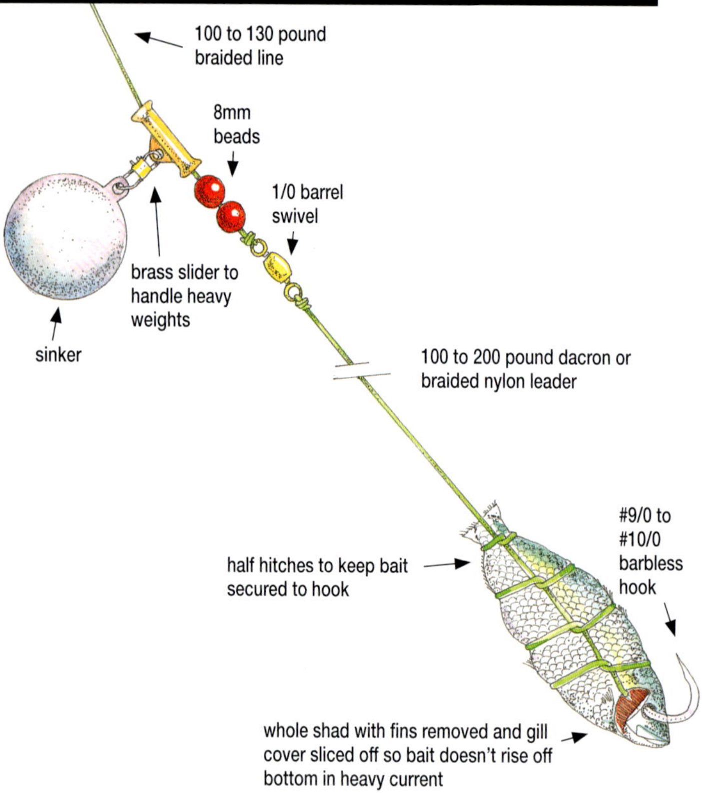

TIP

Quality tackle is required when targeting surgeon, it needs to be up to the job of catching these big fish. While various baits such as lamprey, smelt and squid are often used, whole rigged shad are hard to beat. Shad should be rigged as shown with elasticized sewing thread or half hitches, with anglers paying particular attention to keep the hook point well exposed to facilitate a good hookup.

BANK BREAKAWAY RIG

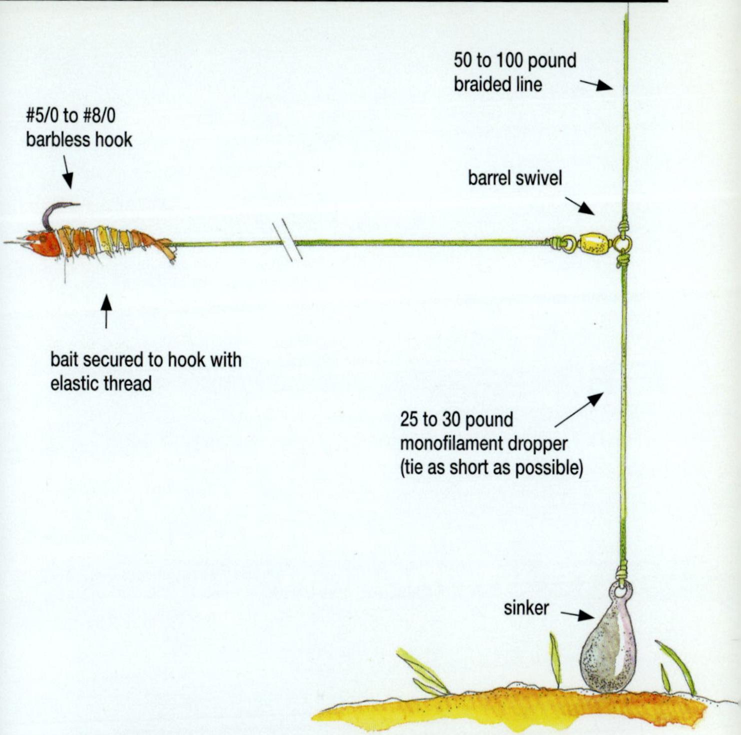

TIP

This is a great rig to use from shore. Use elasticized thread to secure the bait. The idea of using a lighter dropper line to the sinker is so that the sinker will lodge in rocks on the bottom of the river and allow the bait to float in the current, when a fish takes the bait and you strike, the sacrificial dropper line will break off.

SOFT BOTTOM ESTUARY RIG

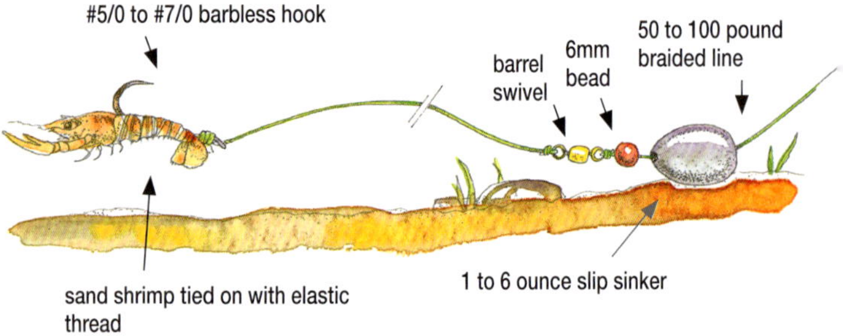

TIP

Where the bottom is mostly mud and sand, a basic running sinker rig is all that is required, and it's a simple rig to tie. The weight of the sinker you use should be determined by the strength of the tidal current.

WHITE STURGEON

Its sheer size alone makes it a tough adversary. It is a strong fighter that often jumps or rolls on the anglers line to avoid capture. Heavy baitcasting or light saltwater tackle is best used in gentle water, but it may be necessary to go far heavier in fast or deep-water areas. They feed on dead fish, crustaceans, molluscs and baits such as dead shad, smelt anchovies; cut fish, clams, crayfish. Earthworms and shrimp are also effective.

RIGGING Natural live baits

LEARNING HOW TO RIG NATURAL BAITS SO THEY REMAIN ALIVE IS OFTEN THE KEY TO PUTTING MORE FISH IN THE BAG.

FROGS

TIP

Frogs should be hooked lightly through the lip or either of the hind legs so that they can swim about naturally on the surface.

CRICKETS AND GRASSHOPPERS

TIP

Hook lightly through the hard wing case area behind the head to allow the insects to kick about naturally.

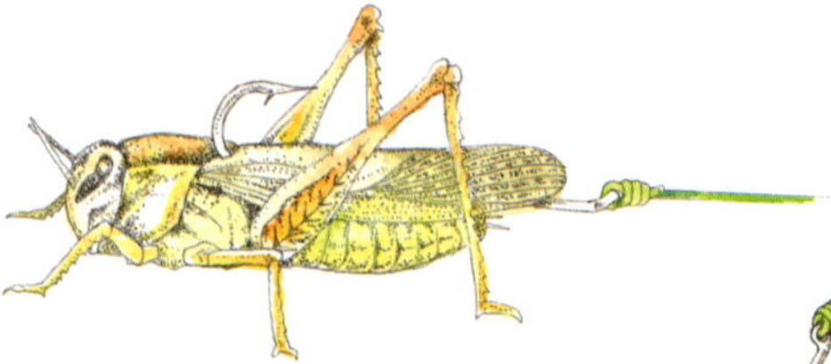

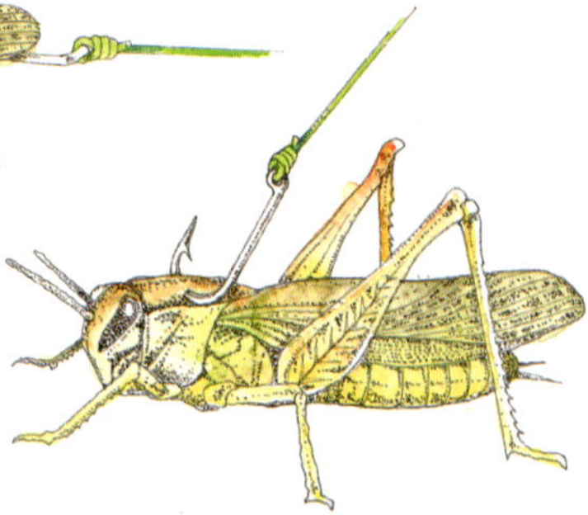

CRAWDADS

TIP

Hook crawdads through the last segment near the tail and with the hook facing up and backwards so that it can move about without hooking up on the bottom.

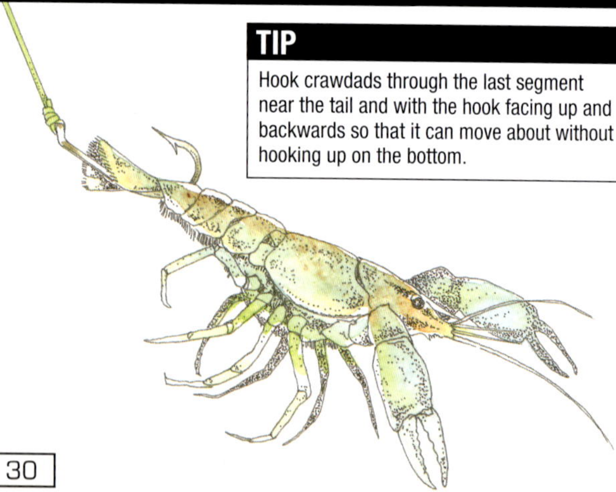

NIGHTCRAWLERS

TIP

There are a number of ways to rig nightcrawlers for fishing under a bobber, on the bottom or as retrieved live bait. Try and leave one or both ends free from the hook to encourage fish attracting movement.

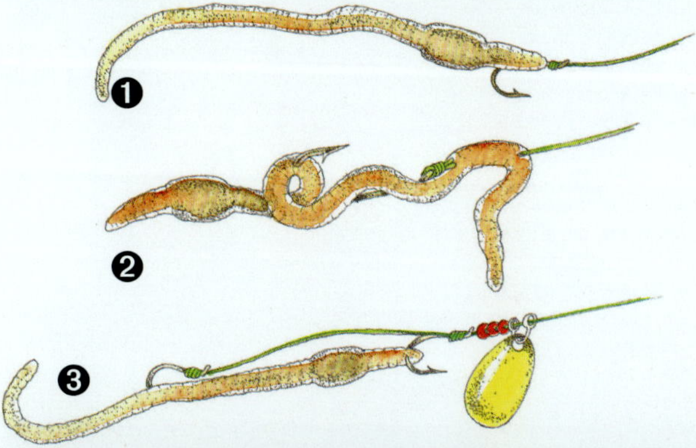

TIP

❶ One of the most natural ways to rig nightcrawlers is to use a light line and small hook and allow the bait to drift naturally with the current flow through a pool. When fishing with this rig the fish will often pick it up as it drifts past in a very natural manner.

❷ The hook should be large enough to enable you to thread the worm onto the hook two or three times while allowing both ends of the worm to be free of the hook to swing about enticingly. Keep the hook size as small as possible to match the fish you're targeting also. If you're using smaller worms then load a few onto a hook so that fish such as catfish and carp have a good 'gob' of worms to eat.

❸ Attaching a spinner blade above a double hook rig can be very enticing to many fish. Rig some coloured beads above the first snelled hook to keep the spinner blade free of the first hook and attach the trail or stinger hook back from the tail of the nightcrawler to allow the tail to flutter about when being cast and retrieved, or trolled.

CATERPILLARS AND SMALLER GRUBS

TIP

Caterpillars can be lightly hooked through the skin, while smaller, more delicate grubs can be attached to the hook with stretch thread. The key to fishing any small grubs is to use the appropriate hook size for the bait. Using chemically sharpened hooks also allows more hook ups. Caterpillars have tough skins so hooking directly through the back is the way to go, but when you're rigging delicate, small insects and grubs to very small hooks it often pays to use elasticized sewing thread to attach them to the hook rather than risk tearing the bait with the hook when rigging or casting.

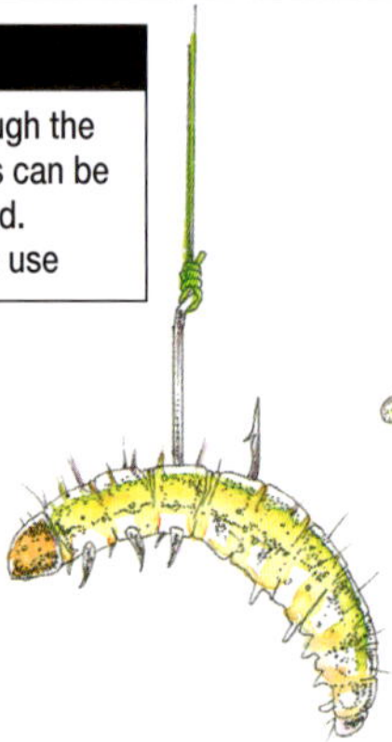

MINNOWS

TIP

Minnows can be rigged on hooks with 'weed guards', or on small jig heads to fish amongst structure. Try rigging a spinner blade in front to increase the baits appeal from a distance when trolling.

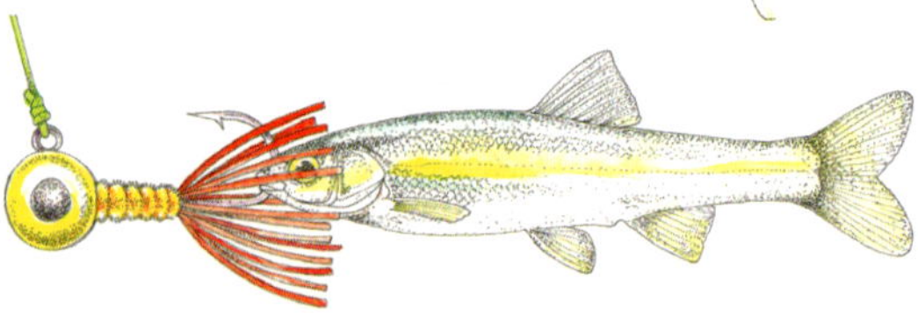